# LITTLE KIDS FIRST BIG BOOK OF SPACE

BY CATHERINE D. HUGHES

ILLUSTRATED BY DAVID A. AGUILAR

NATIONAL GEOGRAPHIC KIDS

WASHINGTON, D.C.

# CONTENTS

Introduction: How to Use This Book
**6**

Our Solar System
**8**

## LOOKING UP FROM EARTH 10

## EARTH'S NEIGHBORHOOD 32

## EARTH'S OTHER NEIGHBORS 70

## FAR, FAR AWAY 88

## EXPLORING SPACE 106

Solar System Map
**120**

Parent Tips
**122**

Glossary
**124**

Index
**126**

# INTRODUCTION

This book is an introduction to space and all that is in it. It answers questions from "How many stars are there?" to "What is space?"

When we look up at the sky, we see the moon, the sun and other stars, and vast areas of nothing. Between the stars, planets, and moons, and beyond any atmospheres they might have, there are occasional chunks of rock and metal, a lot of dust, and many gases. The vast "nothing" in between all those things is space.

**NATIONAL GEOGRAPHIC LITTLE KIDS FIRST BIG BOOK OF SPACE IS DIVIDED INTO FIVE CHAPTERS.**

**CHAPTER ONE** begins the book with a few of the more familiar parts of space—the sun, Earth, moon, and meteors.

In **CHAPTER TWO,** the journey of discovery continues through the solar system to the seven other big planets—Venus, Mercury, Mars, Saturn, Jupiter, Neptune, and Uranus.

Other solar system neighbors are introduced in **CHAPTER THREE**— asteroids, dwarf planets (bringing the number of planets in our solar system to 13), and comets.

In **CHAPTER FOUR,** moving farther into space, the book covers such topics as the universe and its stars, constellations, galaxies, nebulae, and mysterious black holes.

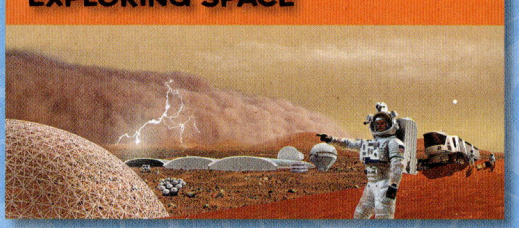

**CHAPTER FIVE** introduces the ways people explore space, featuring spaceships, telescopes, and space stations. You can even explore a futuristic settlement on Mars!

# HOW TO USE THIS BOOK

**POP-UP FACTS** sprinkled throughout provide added information and build on the main text in each section.

**FACT BOXES** give the young reader a quick overview of each topic. The size of Earth (always on the left) is shown in relation to planets. The distance from Earth is given as the time it has taken spacecraft to reach each place for a flyby.

The huge **VOLCANOES** on Mars may be the **BIGGEST** in the **SOLAR SYSTEM**.

Deimos

One day on Mars is about the **SAME LENGTH OF TIME** as one day on Earth.

Phobos

## EARTH'S NEIGHBORHOOD

# MARS

Mars is more like Earth than any other planet in the solar system.

Scientists think there may have been flowing rivers on Mars long ago. They are curious about where the river water is now. It may be frozen beneath the surface.

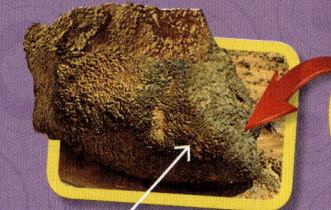

**FACTS**

**SIZE**
Earth  Mars

**SAY MY NAME**
MARS

**PLACE IN SPACE**
Fourth planet in orbit around the sun

**HOW FAR AWAY**
It takes eight months for a spaceship to get there.

Mars looks reddish because there is a lot of **IRON** in the **ROCKS** on its surface. **IRON** is a **METAL THAT RUSTS**, turning red.

Colorful art and crisp photographs illustrate the topics on every spread, supported by captions that further explain details.

**MORE FOR PARENTS**
In the back of the book you will find a map of the solar system, parent tips with fun space activities, and a helpful glossary.

# OUR SOLAR SYSTEM

Note: Distances between planets are not to scale.

The sun is the center of Earth's solar system. The book begins with this important star. This artwork shows the size of the sun compared to the eight big planets, five dwarf planets, and several moons that you will read about in chapters 1, 2, and 3. The locations of the asteroid belt and the Kuiper belt are also shown. Refer back to this artwork as you read about each topic.

# CHAPTER ONE  LOOKING

The sun sets as the moon rises over planet Earth.

# UP FROM EARTH

This blast from the surface of the sun is called a solar flare.

**LOOKING UP FROM EARTH**

# SUN

The sun is a star. It is the closest star to Earth, the planet you live on. The sun is very hot. Its warmth and light keep plants and animals on Earth alive, including you.

The sun, planets, moons, and different kinds of space rocks are all part of our solar system. The sun is at the center of this solar system.

**THE SUN** is about **93 MILLION MILES** away from **EARTH.**

If you could **DRIVE** to the sun in a car, it would take **MORE THAN 170 YEARS** to get there.

Earth travels around the sun in a big circle called an orbit. It takes a whole year for Earth to travel all the way around the sun. A year on Earth is the time it takes Earth to orbit the sun.

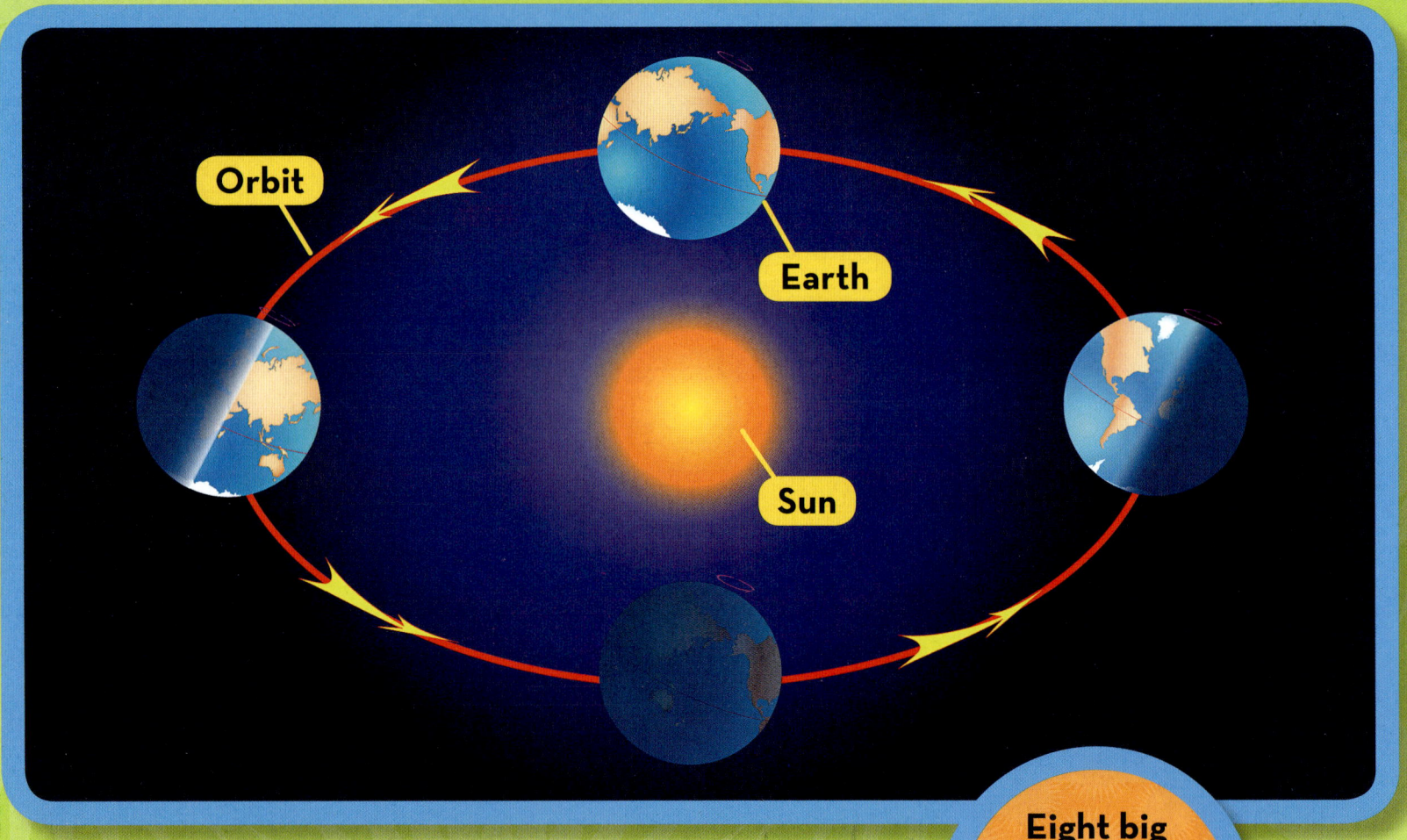

**How many times have you been all the way around the sun?**
(HINT: How many years old are you?)

Eight big **PLANETS** orbit the sun, including **EARTH.**

## LOOKING UP FROM EARTH

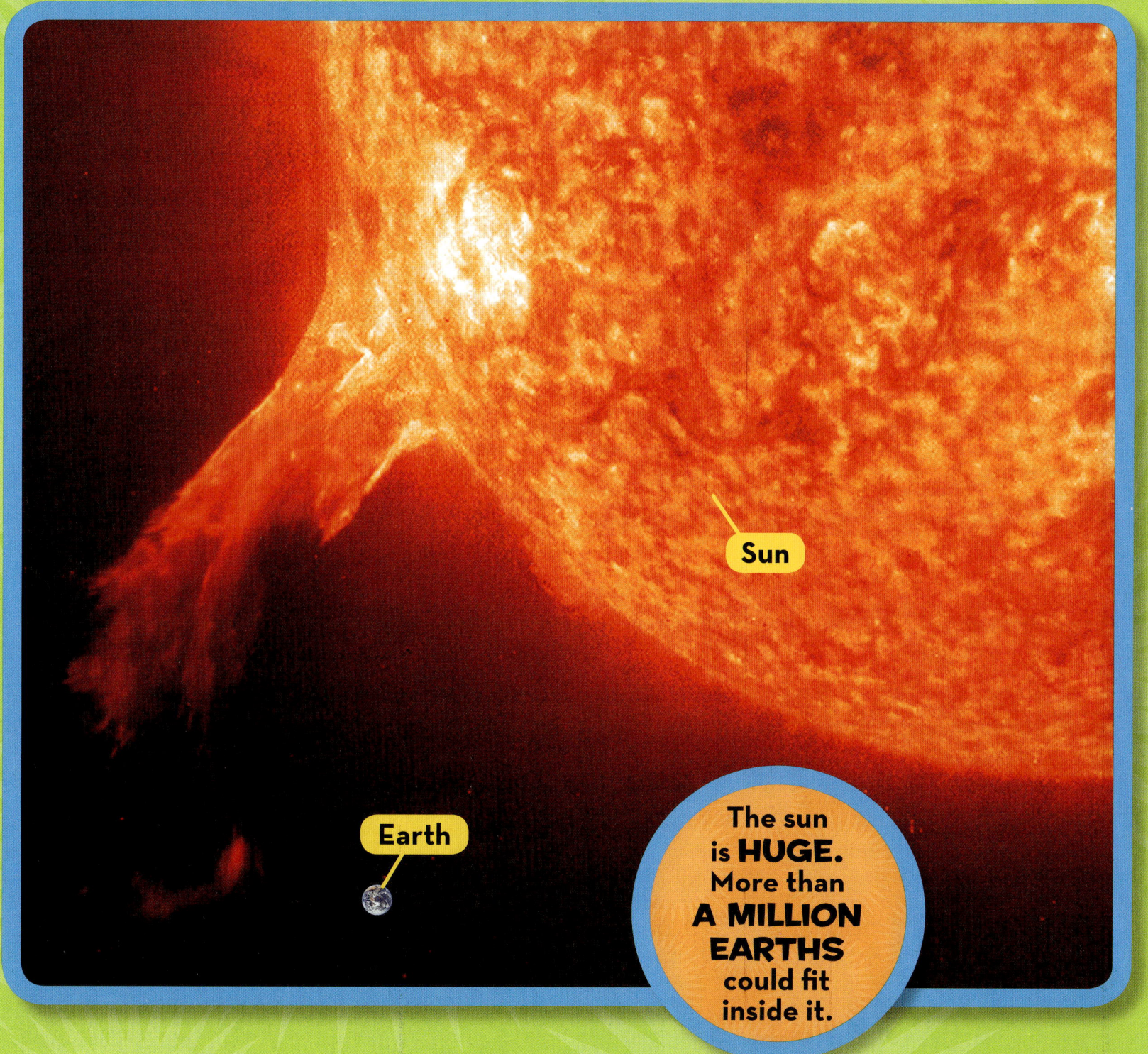

Sun

Earth

The sun is **HUGE.** More than **A MILLION EARTHS** could fit inside it.

During the day, the place where you see the sun changes. In the morning, the sun comes up. This is sunrise, when dark nighttime turns into bright daytime.

You will always see **SUNRISE** in the direction called the **EAST.**

## LOOKING UP FROM EARTH

By lunchtime, the sun is high up in the sky.

In the late afternoon, the sun is low in the sky. Soon it is sunset, as the sun disappears from sight. Then it is nighttime again.

Do not look directly at the **SUN**. It is so **BRIGHT** that it can hurt your eyes.

**SUNSET** is always in the direction called the **WEST**.

Most of **EARTH** is covered by **OCEANS.** The blue areas are water.

Moon

Earth

**EARTH** is the **FIFTH LARGEST PLANET** in the solar system.

**LOOKING UP FROM EARTH**

# EARTH

A planet is a big, round object in space that orbits a star. Earth is your home. The sun is your star.

Earth is always moving. As it orbits the sun, it also spins around like a top.

**EARTH is the THIRD planet in orbit around the SUN.**

**EARTH spins at 1,000 MILES AN HOUR.**

When you spin around on your feet you probably get dizzy. But you cannot feel Earth spin.

During the day it is light outside, and you can see the sun.

As Earth spins, the place where you are on the planet turns away from the sun. That is when it gets dark outside.

As Earth keeps spinning, you soon see the sun again. It takes Earth one day and one night—24 hours—to spin all the way around.

## LOOKING UP FROM EARTH

When it is **SUMMER** where you live, your part of Earth **IS TILTED TOWARD THE SUN.**

When it is **WINTER** where you live, your part of Earth **IS TILTED AWAY FROM THE SUN.**

A strong, invisible force called gravity pulls everything on Earth down. Gravity keeps you—and all the things around you—from floating up into the sky.

When you **JUMP UP** from the ground, **GRAVITY** is what **PULLS YOU BACK DOWN.**

**Can you jump up five times in a row to show that gravity works every time?**

## LOOKING UP FROM EARTH

Earth is a special planet. It is the only place we know of where there is life—plants and animals, including people.

The **JAGUAR** is one of the many kinds of animals that **LIVE ON PLANET EARTH.**

It takes about **27 DAYS** for the **MOON TO ORBIT EARTH.**

## LOOKING UP FROM EARTH

# MOON

You can often spot Earth's moon when you look into the sky at night. The moon orbits Earth, just like Earth orbits the sun. The moon is rocky and cold.

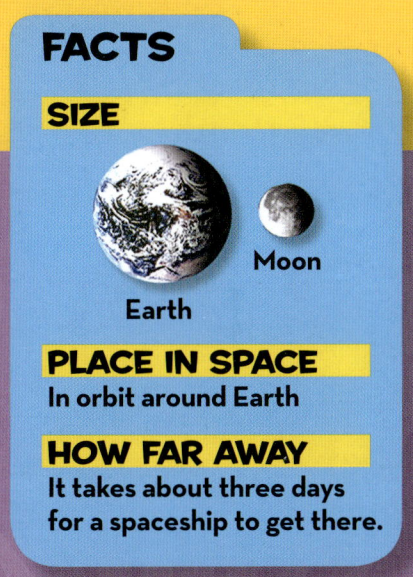

**FACTS**

**SIZE**

Earth — Moon

**PLACE IN SPACE**
In orbit around Earth

**HOW FAR AWAY**
It takes about three days for a spaceship to get there.

The moon looks bright, but it is actually a dark place. It looks bright only when the sun's light reflects, or bounces off, its surface.

The shape of the moon you see changes.
These changes are called the phases of the moon.
The phases change as the moon orbits Earth.

Crescent moon

The MOON is EARTH'S CLOSEST NEIGHBOR in space.

First quarter moon

Sometimes the moon has the shape of a banana.

At other times, it looks like half of a circle.

## LOOKING UP FROM EARTH

There are times when the moon looks almost like a full circle.

About once a month, it looks like a bright, round ball.

Gibbous moon

Full moon

The SAME SIDE OF THE MOON always faces EARTH.

Which phase of the moon is your favorite?

The only place in space on which people have landed is the moon. Before you were born, astronauts—people who travel into space—visited the moon.

Moon lander

Astronauts landed on the moon six times. You can see where in the picture above.

**A MOON LANDER** carried astronauts to the surface of the moon from a bigger spacecraft that stayed in orbit.

## LOOKING UP FROM EARTH

Earth is surrounded by air called the atmosphere. The moon has no atmosphere. An astronaut on the moon must wear a space suit. The space suit has air to breathe. It also keeps the astronaut warm.

Some astronauts who visited the moon had a moon buggy called a **LUNAR ROVING VEHICLE.**

**LOOKING UP FROM EARTH**

# METEORS AND METEORITES

Many chunks of rock float around in space. Sometimes one zooms into Earth's atmosphere toward the planet's surface. That rock is called a meteor.

Usually a meteor burns up before it can reach the ground. But sometimes a meteor reaches Earth's surface. If it hits the ground, it is called a meteorite.

Most meteorites are **SMALL** enough **TO FIT IN YOUR HAND.**

**Do you think it would be fun to watch the night sky for meteors?**

# CHAPTER TWO

Earth has several other planets as neighbors.

# EARTH'S NEIGHBORHOOD

### EARTH'S NEIGHBORHOOD

# ROCKY PLANETS AND GAS GIANTS

To be called a planet, an object has to be round, and it must orbit a star. Nothing else has its exact same orbit. There are eight big planets that orbit the sun.

The four planets closest to the sun are made mostly of rock. They are called terrestrial, or rocky, planets.

The four planets farthest from the sun are big balls of gas. They do not have a solid surface.

Some things are **SOLID**, like a **ROCK**.

Other things are **GAS**, like the **AIR** you breathe.

And some things are **LIQUID**, like **WATER**.

Can you say the names of all eight big planets on page 34?

**EARTH'S NEIGHBORHOOD**

# MERCURY

Mercury is the planet closest to the sun. It is the smallest of the eight big planets.

It orbits the sun faster than any other planet. One year on Earth, the time it takes to orbit the sun, is 365 days. One year on Mercury is only 88 days.

**FACTS**

**SIZE**
Earth — Mercury

**SAY MY NAME**
MER-cyu-ree

**PLACE IN SPACE**
First planet in orbit around the sun

**HOW FAR AWAY**
It takes five months for a spaceship to get there.

Mercury
Earth's moon

**MERCURY is only a LITTLE BIGGER than EARTH'S MOON.**

During the day on Mercury, it gets very hot. At night, it gets very cold.

Scientists from the National Aeronautics and Space Administration (NASA) sent a spaceship called MESSENGER to Mercury. NASA is the space program for the United States.

Mercury

MESSENGER

**MESSENGER** traveled 4.9 billion miles (7.9 billion kilometers) before it began to **ORBIT MERCURY.**

A special **SUNSHADE HELPED PROTECT** MESSENGER from the sun's heat as it orbited Mercury.

# EARTH'S NEIGHBORHOOD

This is a **CRATER**. A crater is a **BIG, BOWL-SHAPED HOLE** on the surface of a planet or moon.

This is one of the **PHOTOGRAPHS** that **MESSENGER** took of the **SURFACE OF MERCURY**.

In March 2011, MESSENGER became the first spacecraft to orbit Mercury. MESSENGER sent photographs of Mercury to scientists on Earth.

How old were you when MESSENGER began to orbit Mercury?

MERCURY and VENUS are the only big planets in our solar system that DO NOT HAVE MOONS.

VENUS is the planet CLOSEST TO EARTH.

**EARTH'S NEIGHBORHOOD**

# VENUS

Venus is the hottest planet in our solar system. It has an atmosphere of thick clouds. The clouds hold in heat like a blanket, making Venus very hot.

**FACTS**

**SIZE**

Earth   Venus

**SAY MY NAME**
VEE-nus

**PLACE IN SPACE**
Second planet in orbit around the sun

**HOW FAR AWAY**
It takes about four months for a spaceship to get there.

The sun's light reflects off Venus's clouds. That makes Venus look very bright. Only the moon is brighter in Earth's night sky.

**Can you find Venus in the sky?**
HINT: It looks like the brightest star in the sky. But it is a planet, not a star.

**MAGELLAN** was carried from Earth into space by another spacecraft called the **SPACE SHUTTLE.**

Magellan, a spaceship sent to Venus, was able to peek beneath the planet's thick clouds. It took photographs of the surface of Venus.

One day on **VENUS** is much longer than one day on Earth because Venus **SPINS MORE SLOWLY.**

Earth

Magellan

42

# EARTH'S NEIGHBORHOOD

Magellan showed that most of Venus is covered in lava, the rocks that come from volcanoes.

This is a **VOLCANO** on Venus called **MAAT MONS.**

**EARTH** spins **COUNTER-CLOCKWISE,** or toward the left. **VENUS** spins **CLOCKWISE,** or toward the right.

**VENUS SPINS** in the **OPPOSITE DIRECTION** that **EARTH SPINS.**

EARTH'S NEIGHBORHOOD

# MARS

Mars is more like Earth than any other planet in the solar system.

Scientists think there may have been flowing rivers on Mars long ago. They are curious about where the river water is now. It may be frozen beneath the surface.

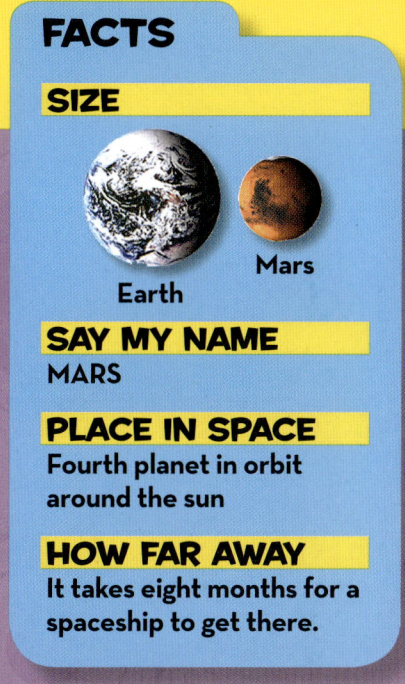

**FACTS**

**SIZE**

Earth   Mars

**SAY MY NAME**
MARS

**PLACE IN SPACE**
Fourth planet in orbit around the sun

**HOW FAR AWAY**
It takes eight months for a spaceship to get there.

Mars looks reddish because there is a lot of **IRON** in the **ROCKS** on its surface. **IRON** is a **METAL THAT RUSTS,** turning red.

45

Mars has two very small moons. They are shaped like potatoes. The moons are called Phobos and Deimos.

**Phobos**

**Deimos**

Pretend you are standing on Phobos. When you look up, Mars would cover a huge part of the sky. That's because Mars is so close to its moon.

## EARTH'S NEIGHBORHOOD

Now pretend you are standing on Earth's moon. When you look up, Earth does not cover as much of the sky. That's because Earth is far away from its moon.

Several spaceships have traveled to Mars carrying equipment to explore the planet. Robots called rovers roll across the surface taking photographs, looking for water, and studying rocks.

The rover **SOJOURNER** was the **FIRST VEHICLE** with **WHEELS** used to **EXPLORE** another planet.

Sojourner

The rover **SPIRIT** took this photograph of the **SURFACE OF MARS.**

Victoria crater

## EARTH'S NEIGHBORHOOD

Two rovers called Spirit and Opportunity landed on two sides of Mars in January 2004. Spirit stopped working in 2010. But Opportunity kept going, continuing to send information back to Earth.

**Did Spirit and Opportunity land on Mars before or after you were born?**

Curiosity

A rover called **CURIOSITY** was **LAUNCHED** from **EARTH** in 2011 to land on Mars in 2012. One of its jobs: **PICK UP** and look at **ROCKS** on **MARS**.

EARTH'S NEIGHBORHOOD

# JUPITER

Jupiter is our solar system's biggest planet. It is so big that all the other planets in the solar system could fit inside it.

**FACTS**

**SIZE**

Earth — Jupiter

**SAY MY NAME**
JOO-peh-ter

**PLACE IN SPACE**
Fifth planet in orbit around the sun

**HOW FAR AWAY**
It takes 13 months for a spaceship to get there.

It takes almost **12 EARTH YEARS** for **JUPITER** to completely **ORBIT THE SUN.**

The huge storm on Jupiter is called the Great Red Spot. The storm is like a hurricane on Earth, but Jupiter's storm has been blowing for hundreds of years!

**What kinds of storms do you have where you live?**

Earth has one moon. Mars has two moons. Jupiter has at least sixty-three moons! Jupiter's four biggest moons are Europa, Callisto, Io, and Ganymede.

**EUROPA** may have a deep, **ICE-COVERED OCEAN.**

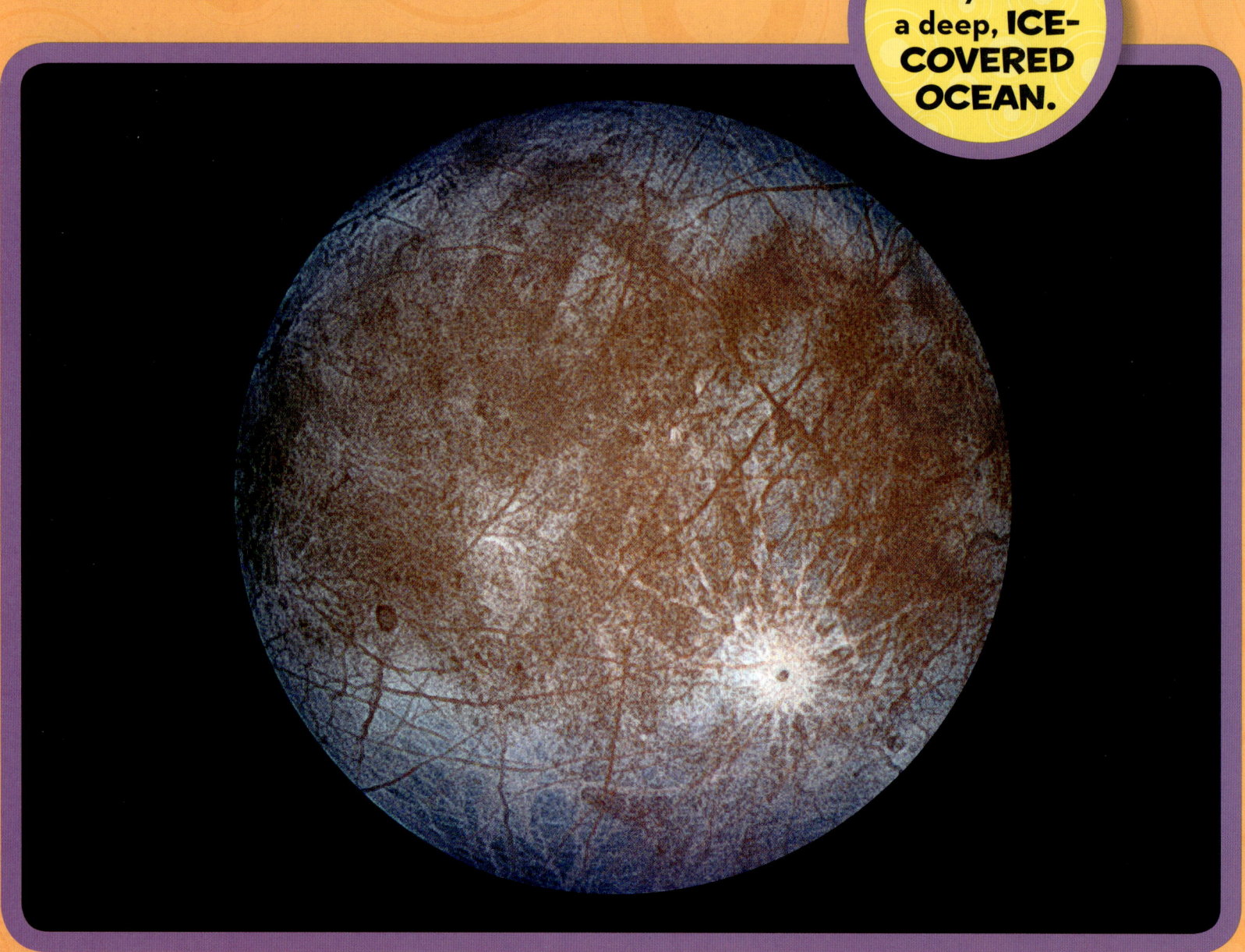

# EARTH'S NEIGHBORHOOD

The moon **CALLISTO** and the planet **MERCURY** are about the **SAME SIZE**.

The moon **IO** is covered by **ACTIVE** volcanoes.

Scientists are very curious about Europa. Ice covers its surface. Scientists think that there may be an ocean underneath the ice.

**GANYMEDE** is the **BIGGEST MOON** in our whole solar system.

Jupiter

Galileo

GALILEO SENT BACK thousands of PHOTOGRAPHS of Jupiter.

A spaceship named Galileo carried a smaller spacecraft called a probe. The probe went down into Jupiter's atmosphere. It measured temperatures and other things for about an hour before it was destroyed by storms.

## EARTH'S NEIGHBORHOOD

JUNO reached JUPITER in 2016.

A spacecraft called Juno is filled with instruments that send information back to scientists on Earth. It is the first spacecraft to see beneath the thick clouds that surround Jupiter.

SATURN has thousands of rings.

**EARTH'S NEIGHBORHOOD**

# SATURN

Look at the sparkly rings around Saturn! Saturn's rings are the biggest and brightest in our solar system.

The rings are made up of billions of bits of icy rocks. Some bits are as tiny as specks of dust. Others are the size of huge mountains.

**FACTS**

**SIZE**

Earth

Saturn

**SAY MY NAME**
SAH-tern

**PLACE IN SPACE**
Sixth planet in orbit around the sun

**HOW FAR AWAY**
It takes four years for a spaceship to get there.

**SUNLIGHT REFLECTS OFF THE ICE** in Saturn's rings and makes them **SPARKLE.**

SATURN has at least **53 MOONS.** Here are just a few.

## EARTH'S NEIGHBORHOOD

Saturn's biggest moon is called Titan. The word "titan" means giant. Titan is bigger than the planet Mercury.

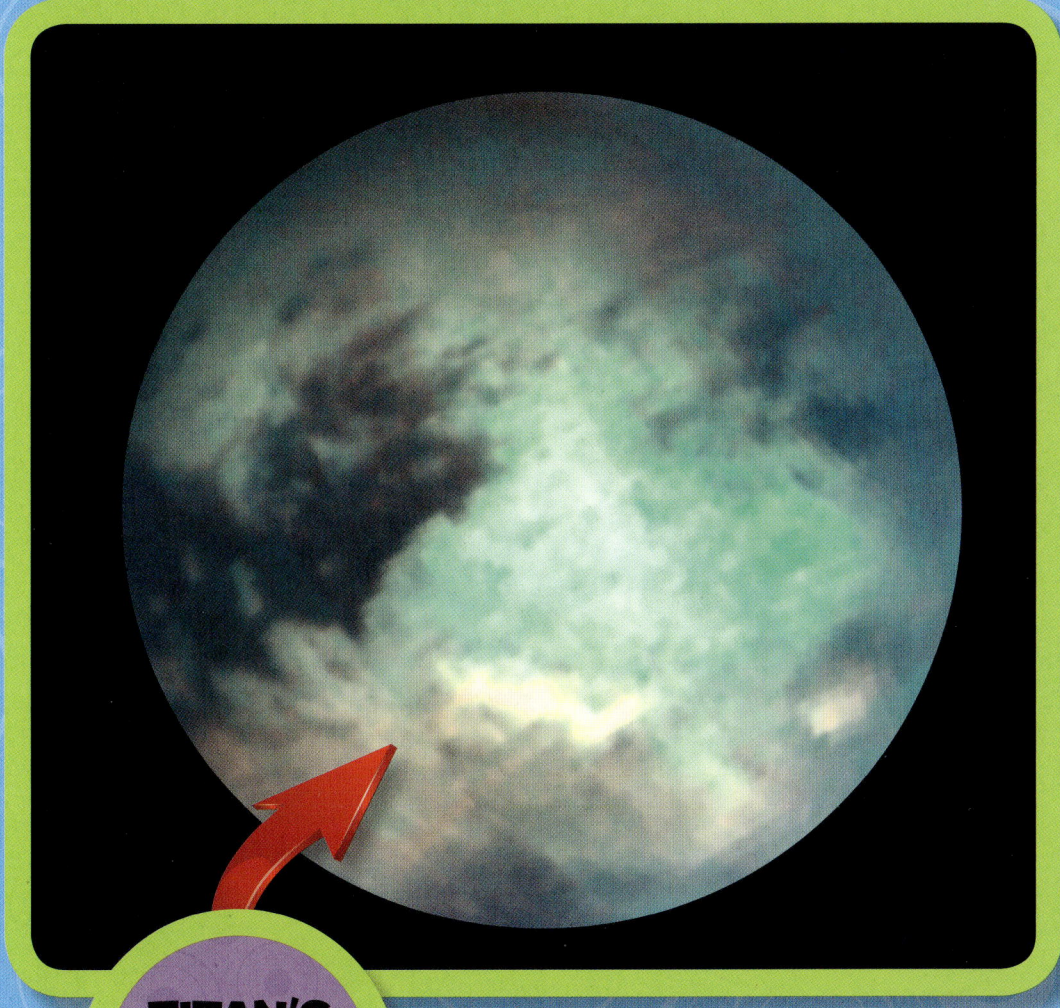

**TITAN'S** surface is **FROZEN.**

Saturn also has several very small moons. Walking all the way around one of the smallest moons would only take as long as walking around five city blocks.

**If you could name a moon, what would you call it?**

A spacecraft called Cassini reached Saturn in 2004. It was the first to orbit Saturn, and it will continue its orbit until 2017.

When a spacecraft **FLIES BY A PLANET OR MOON** without **GOING INTO ORBIT AROUND IT,** the flight is called a **FLYBY.**

An **ORBITER** is a spacecraft that stays in orbit around a **PLANET OR MOON.**

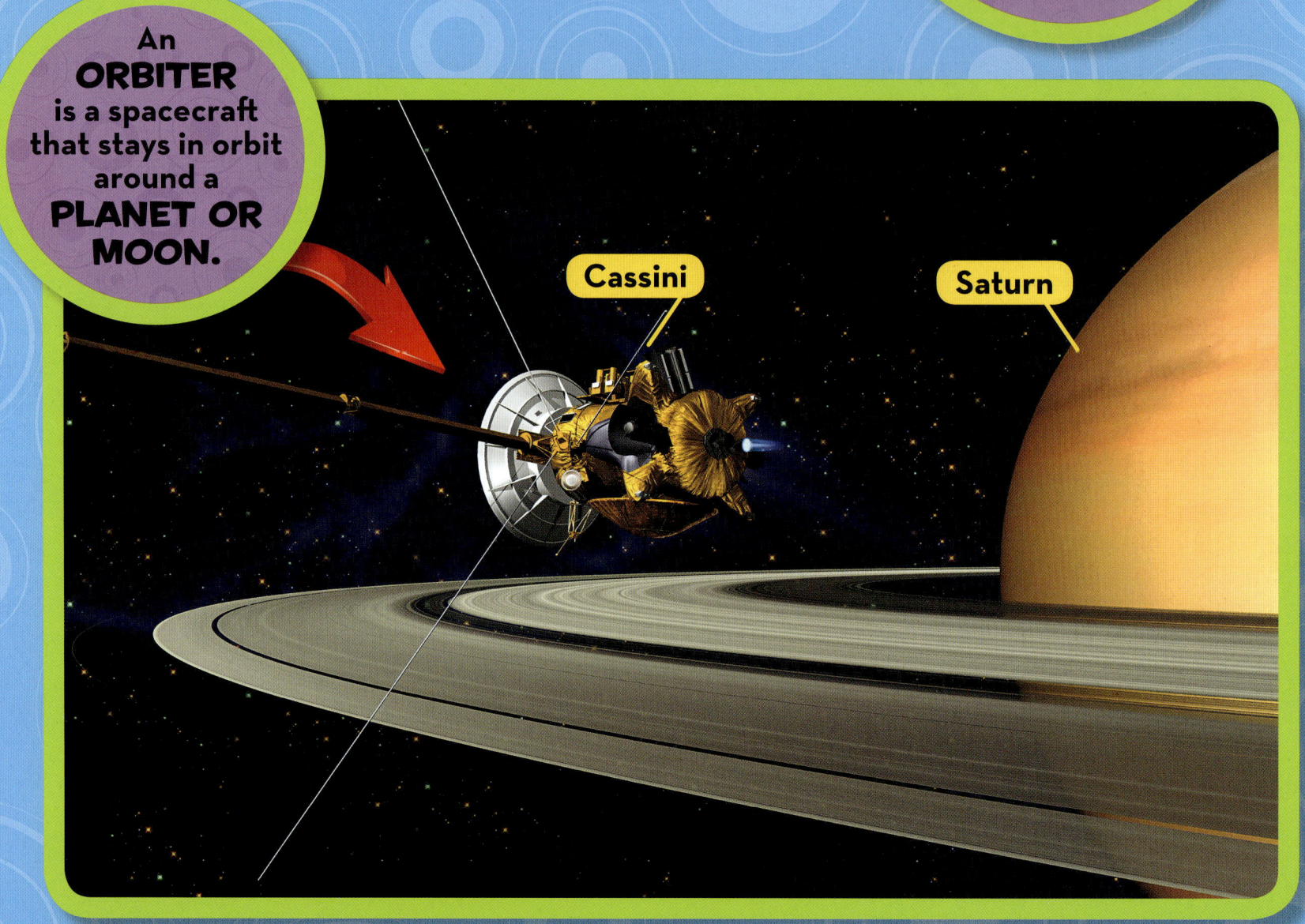

## EARTH'S NEIGHBORHOOD

On board Cassini was a lander called Huygens (HOY-gans). It launched from Cassini to land on Titan. A parachute helped Huygens float to the surface.

Parachute

Huygens

Titan

Huygens on Titan

A **LANDER** is a spacecraft that lands on the surface of a **MOON OR PLANET.**

It takes **84 EARTH YEARS** for Uranus to orbit the sun.

**URANUS SPINS** in the **OPPOSITE** direction that **EARTH** does.

**EARTH'S NEIGHBORHOOD**

# URANUS

Uranus is tipped onto its side. Scientists think that a long time ago some huge space object, the size of a planet, may have crashed into Uranus. That crash caused Uranus to tip.

Compare the pictures of Saturn and Uranus, below. Do you see how Uranus looks tipped?

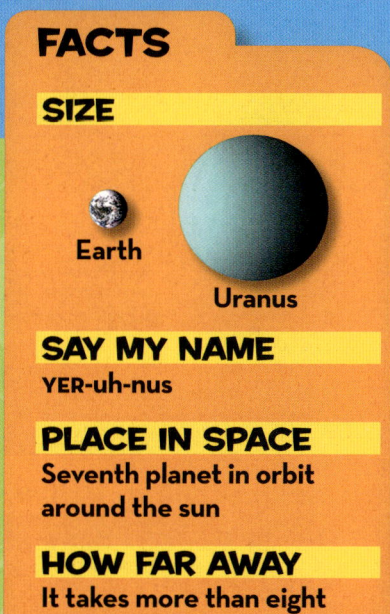

**FACTS**

**SIZE**
Earth — Uranus

**SAY MY NAME**
YER-uh-nus

**PLACE IN SPACE**
Seventh planet in orbit around the sun

**HOW FAR AWAY**
It takes more than eight years for a spaceship to get there.

Saturn — Uranus

Icy Uranus is the coldest of the eight big planets.

Uranus

URANUS has at least 13 rings, but they are very hard to see.

Miranda

One MOON orbiting Uranus is named MIRANDA.

Can you count to 27?

No one knows for sure how many moons orbit Uranus, but it has at least 27. There may be more that people who study space, called astronomers, have not yet found.

# EARTH'S NEIGHBORHOOD

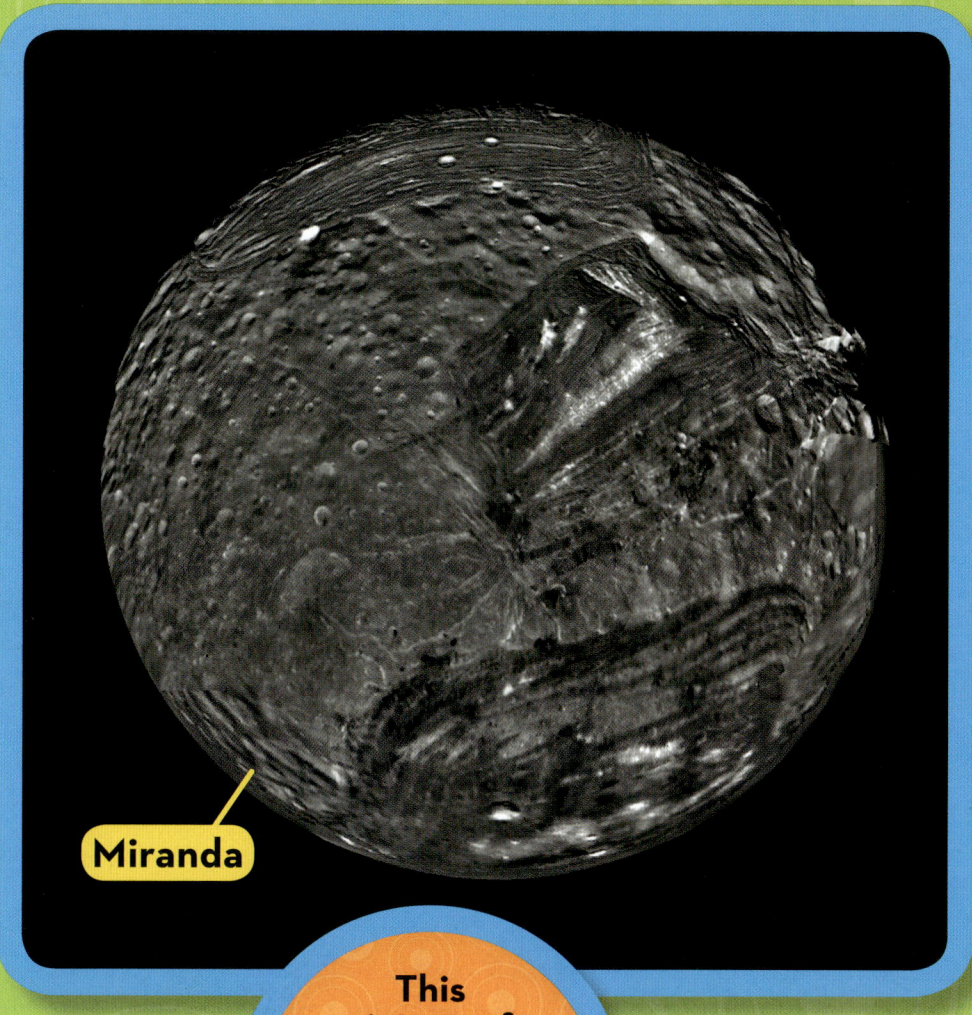

Miranda

A spacecraft called Voyager 2 is the only spacecraft that has flown near Uranus. It was close to the planet for only five-and-a-half hours as it traveled farther into space.

This picture of **MIRANDA** came from **VOYAGER 2.**

**MIRANDA** has a very strange-looking **SURFACE.** It has canyons 12 times deeper than Earth's Grand Canyon.

**EARTH'S NEIGHBORHOOD**

# NEPTUNE

Neptune is farther from the sun than any of the other big planets.

The weather on this planet is wild. Winds blow more than a thousand miles an hour!

Remember the Great Red Spot on Jupiter? Neptune also had a big storm like that. On Neptune, it was called the Great Dark Spot. Neptune has many storms that come and go.

**FACTS**

**SIZE**
Earth
Neptune

**SAY MY NAME**
NEP-tune

**PLACE IN SPACE**
Eighth planet in orbit around the sun

**HOW FAR AWAY**
It takes 12 years for a spaceship to get there.

It takes Neptune **165 YEARS TO TRAVEL** all the way **AROUND THE SUN.**

Triton is Neptune's largest moon. It is one of the coldest places in our solar system.

**NEPTUNE is TOO FAR AWAY TO SEE FROM EARTH without a telescope.**

Triton has volcano-like eruptions that burst from openings in the surface. Gas and dust explode up high, freeze instantly, and fall back down onto the moon like snow.

# EARTH'S NEIGHBORHOOD

After Voyager 2 flew by Uranus, it headed toward Neptune. There it discovered six moons. Seven others had already been found. So Neptune has at least 13 moons.

Cameras

Antenna

**PROTEUS** is Neptune's **SECOND LARGEST** moon. **NEREID** is its **THIRD LARGEST**.

After it flew by Neptune in 1989, **VOYAGER 2** continued on **INTO OUTER SPACE**.

If you could send a spacecraft somewhere in space to take photographs, where would you send it?

# CHAPTER THREE

Asteroids and other objects fly through space.

# EARTH'S OTHER NEIGHBORS

An ARTIST SHOWS what it might look like when two ASTEROIDS CRASH.

**EARTH'S OTHER NEIGHBORS**

# ASTEROID BELT

A ring of rocks orbits the sun between Mars and Jupiter.

The rocks are asteroids. Thousands of them race around the sun in a ring called the asteroid belt.

The **ASTEROID BELT** separates the **ROCKY PLANETS** and the **GAS PLANETS** in space.

Asteroid named Eros

Asteroids are kind of like leftovers. They are the leftover bits and pieces of rock and metal in space that did not become planets or moons.

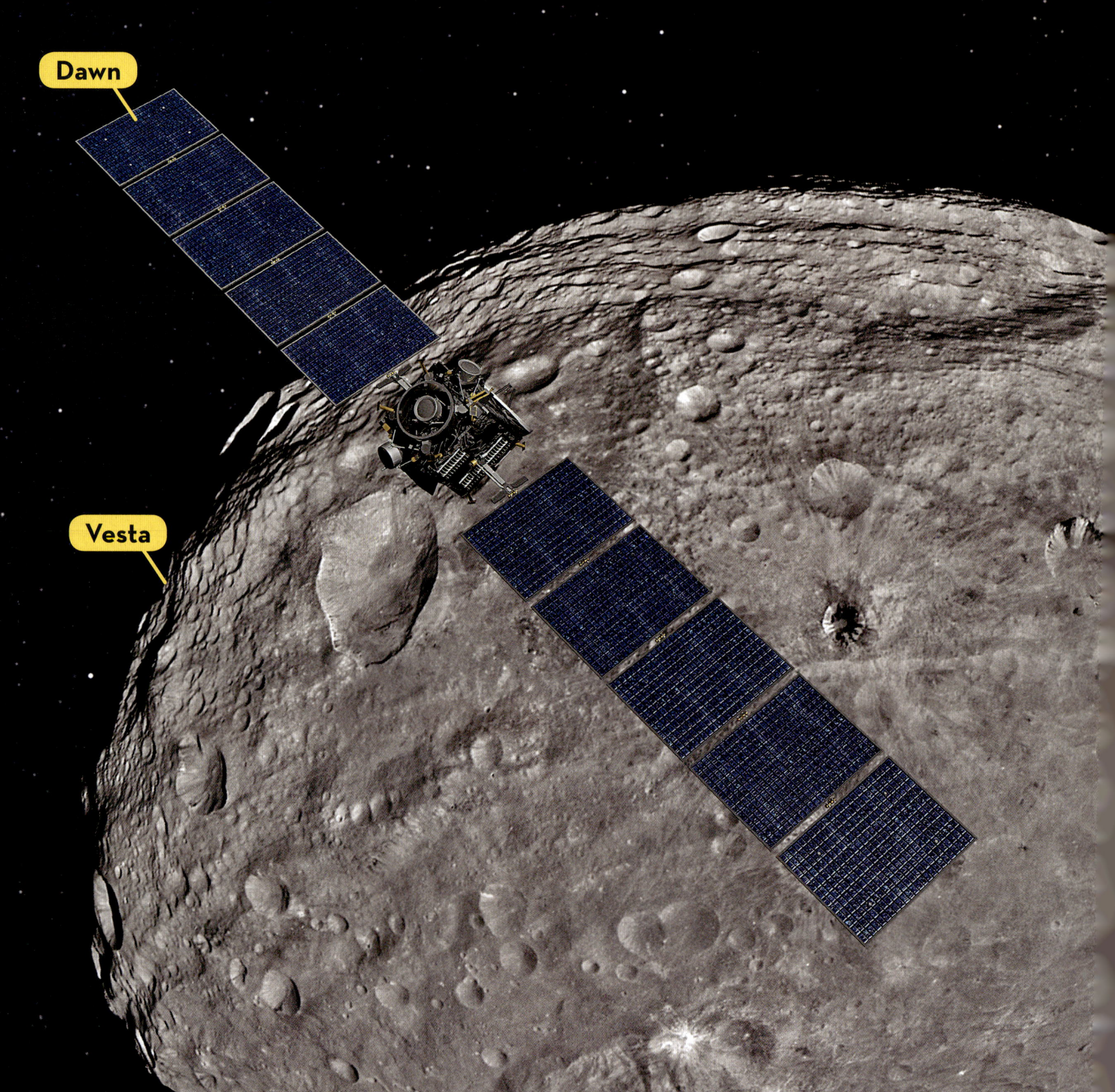

**EARTH'S OTHER NEIGHBORS**

# ASTEROIDS UP CLOSE

Most asteroids are quite small. Some are less than a mile around, while others are more than 500 miles (805 km) around.

In 2007, scientists at NASA sent a spaceship named Dawn to an asteroid called Vesta.

Turn the page to find out where Dawn went next.

One **ASTEROID, NAMED IDA,** surprised scientists by having a **MOON,** which they named **DACTYL.**

If you could name a spaceship, what would you call it?

EARTH'S OTHER NEIGHBORS

# CERES

The word "dwarf" means small. Dwarf planets in our solar system are smaller than the eight big planets. Ceres is one of five dwarf planets.

Dawn, the spaceship you read about on page 75, is now in orbit around Ceres. It arrived there in 2015. With Dawn's help, scientists hope to learn more about asteroids and dwarf planets.

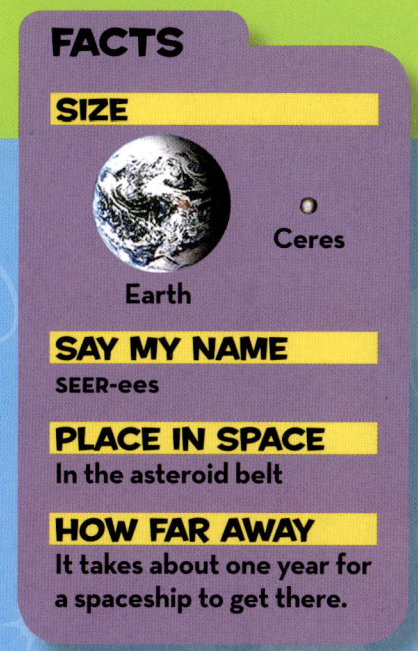

**FACTS**

**SIZE**
Earth — Ceres

**SAY MY NAME**
SEER-ees

**PLACE IN SPACE**
In the asteroid belt

**HOW FAR AWAY**
It takes about one year for a spaceship to get there.

**DAWN** is as big as an **18-WHEEL TRUCK.**

Counting big planets plus dwarf planets, how many planets are there? HINT: 8 + 5 = ?

It takes **PLUTO 248 YEARS** to **ORBIT THE SUN.**

Charon

Pluto

**EARTH'S OTHER NEIGHBORS**

# PLUTO

Far beyond the asteroid belt and Ceres, and past Neptune, is another belt of objects. It is called the Kuiper (KIE-per) belt. This is where you can find the dwarf planet Pluto.

Pluto used to be called a planet. When your parents were in school, they probably learned about *nine* big planets, including Pluto.

But recently scientists decided it is too small. They now say it is a dwarf planet, and that there are only *eight* big planets in our solar system.

**FACTS**

**SIZE**
Earth / Pluto

**SAY MY NAME**
PLOO-tow

**PLACE IN SPACE**
In the Kuiper belt

**HOW FAR AWAY**
It takes more than nine years for a spaceship to get there.

**PLUTO SPINS BACKWARD,** like Uranus and Venus.

The moon Charon is about half as big as Pluto. That is a very big moon! Pluto has three smaller moons, too.

The same side of Charon always faces Pluto as the moon orbits the planet, just as Earth's moon does.

This shows you how **HUGE PLUTO** would look in the sky if you were standing on Charon.

## EARTH'S OTHER NEIGHBORS

In January 2006 the United States sent a spaceship toward Pluto. It is called New Horizons.

New Horizons reached Pluto in 2015. It sent information back to scientists on Earth. Now it is heading farther into the Kuiper belt.

PLUTO was NAMED by an 11-YEAR-OLD GIRL.

New Horizons

**Can you name two dwarf planets?**

### EARTH'S OTHER NEIGHBORS

# HAUMEA, ERIS, AND MAKEMAKE

Haumea, Eris, and Makemake are three more dwarf planets in the Kuiper belt. Scientists think that a long time ago something smashed into Haumea.

That crash may have caused chunks of Haumea to fly off, becoming the two moons Namaka and Hi'iaka.

**FACTS**

**SIZE**

Earth, Makemake, Haumea, Eris

**SAY MY NAME**
how-MEH-ya; AIR-is; MAH-kee MAH-kee

**PLACE IN SPACE**
In the Kuiper belt

Eris

ERIS is the BIGGEST DWARF PLANET.

It takes MAKEMAKE 310 YEARS to ORBIT the SUN.

Makemake

Can you name all five dwarf planets by heart?

## EARTH'S OTHER NEIGHBORS

# COMETS

A comet is sort of like a huge, dirty snowball. It is made of icy gas and rock. Comets have huge orbits around the sun. Sometimes a comet travels close enough to the sun to begin to melt. When that happens, a tail forms behind it.

A **COMET** that **CRASHES INTO THE SUN** is called a **SUN-GRAZER.**

Tail

A comet's tail can be very long and beautiful. It sometimes stretches for millions of miles.

Some comets are found in the Kuiper belt. They take hundreds of years to orbit the sun.

Other comets are found far beyond Neptune. Those comets can take millions of years to orbit the sun.

A SPACECRAFT called ROSETTA heads toward a COMET.

Rosetta

Comet

Can you pretend that a chair is the sun and that you are a comet in orbit around it?

# EARTH'S OTHER NEIGHBORS

# CHAPTER FOUR

Beautiful stars swirl far, far away.

# FAR, FAR AWAY

**THERE ARE MANY AMAZING THINGS IN THE UNIVERSE.** This photograph shows one called a nebula. You will find out what a nebula is on page 103.

**FAR, FAR AWAY**

# UNIVERSE

The universe is everything in our solar system and outside it. The universe is so huge that it is hard to even imagine its size.

In this chapter you will find out what is beyond our solar system.

**STARS** and **PLANETS** make up other solar systems far from our own.

**If you could travel anywhere in the universe, where would you most like to visit?**

STARS come in DIFFERENT SIZES and COLORS.

Hot star

Cool star

Can you draw and color a star of each temperature?

**FAR, FAR AWAY**

# STARS

On a clear night, with no clouds or city lights, you can see about 3,000 stars in the sky. But there are billions more that you cannot see.

Stars create energy that makes them shine. They are made of hot gases that are held together by the star's gravity.

**STARS HAVE DIFFERENT TEMPERATURES.** The hottest stars are blue. The coolest stars are red. Yellow stars, like Earth's sun, have a temperature between blue and red stars.

Hottest — In-between — Coolest

The closest star to Earth is the sun. It takes about eight minutes for the sun's light to reach Earth.

SUNLIGHT makes BUBBLES SPARKLE!

# FAR, FAR AWAY

The next closest star to Earth is Proxima-Centauri. Light from that star takes more than four years to reach Earth.

It would take 19,000 years for a spacecraft to reach Proxima-Centauri from Earth. So even though it's the next closest star to Earth, it is very far away!

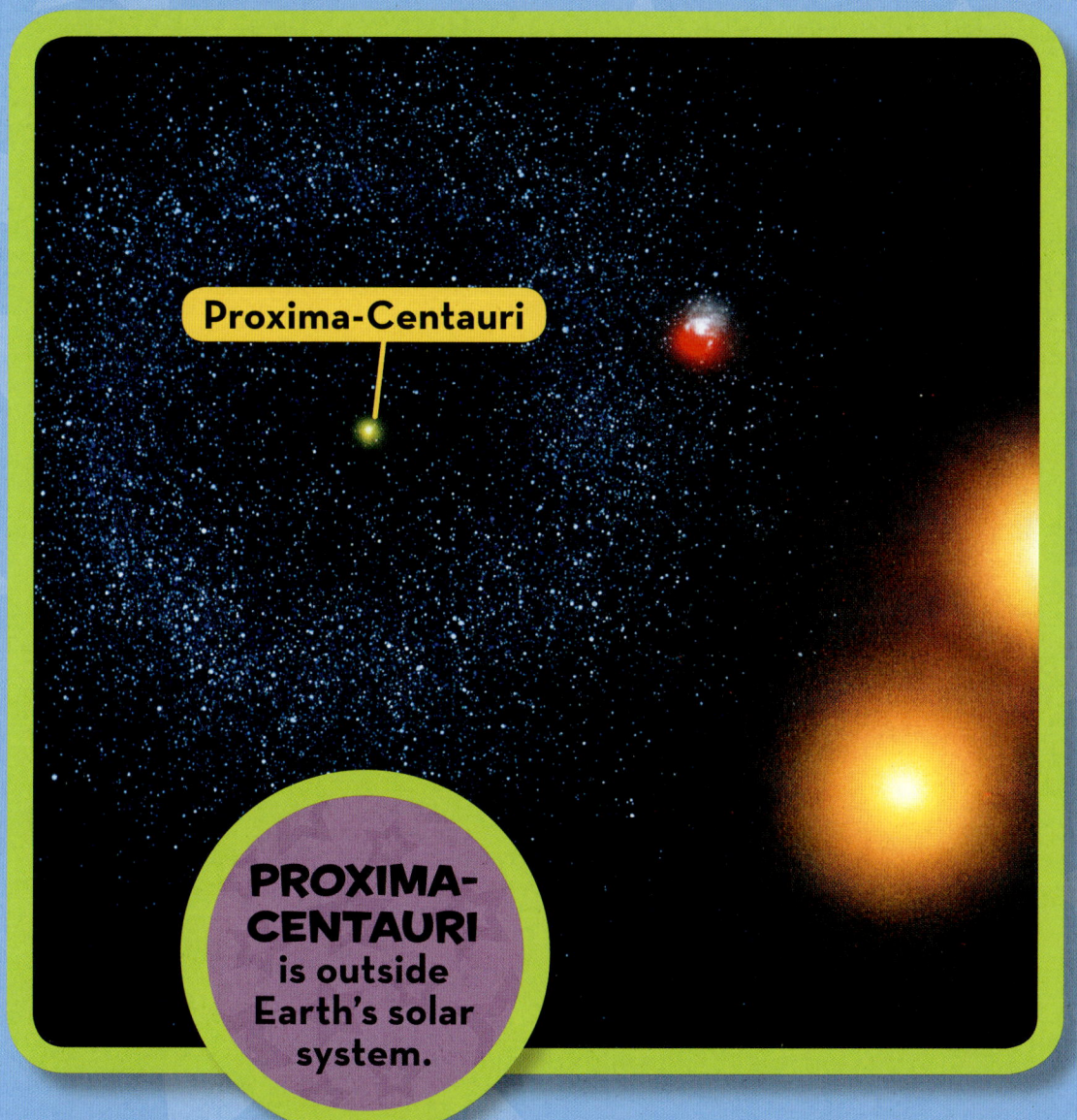

Proxima-Centauri

**PROXIMA-CENTAURI** is outside Earth's solar system.

**FAR, FAR AWAY**

# CONSTELLATIONS

For a long time, people have drawn imaginary, or pretend, lines from star to star, creating pictures in groups of stars. These groups are called constellations.

When you look up at the starry sky, can you imagine your own dot-to-dot pictures?

Constellations are like maps in the sky. There are 88 of them.

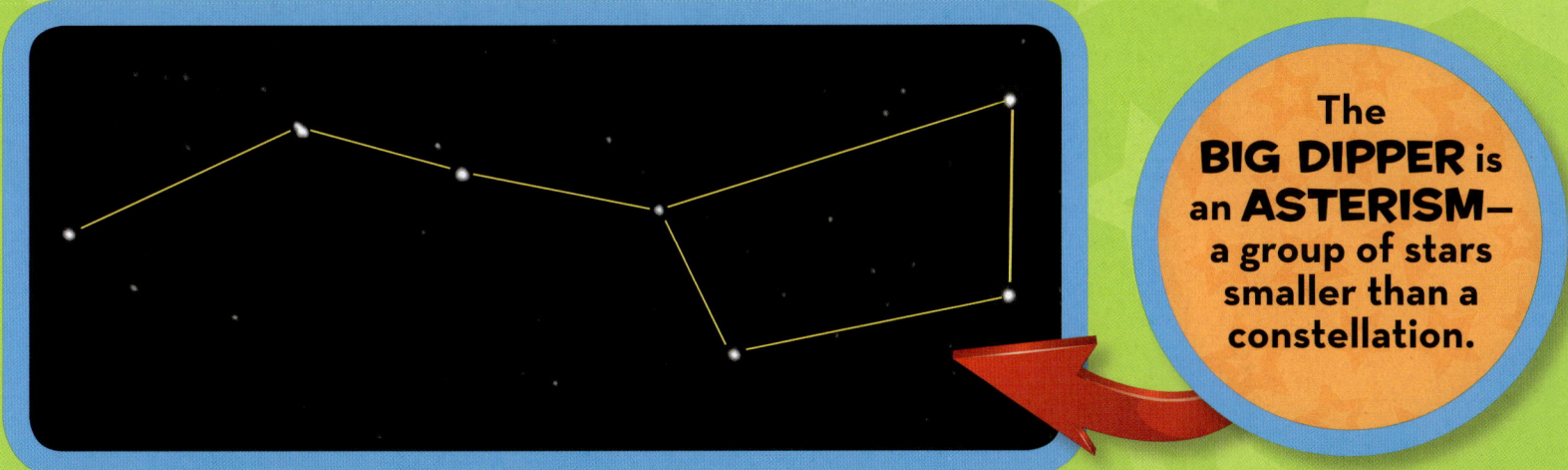

The **BIG DIPPER** is an **ASTERISM**—a group of stars smaller than a constellation.

There are **BILLIONS** of **GALAXIES** in the universe.

**SPIRAL** galaxies are the shape of a **PINWHEEL**.

FAR, FAR AWAY

# GALAXIES

A galaxy is a group of stars, gas, and dust held together by gravity. Galaxies have different shapes. Here are photographs of the three main kinds: spiral, irregular, and elliptical.

**ELLIPTICAL** galaxies are **EGG-SHAPED.**

**IRREGULAR** galaxies **DO NOT** have a particular **SHAPE.**

**Which kind of galaxy do you like the best?**

**FAR, FAR AWAY**

# MILKY WAY

Earth is in a galaxy called the Milky Way. It is a spiral galaxy.

The Milky Way is huge. There are billions of stars in the Milky Way. (That's a lot!)

Earth

**EARTH** is located right here, on one of the **MILKY WAY'S ARMS.**

The **ANDROMEDA** galaxy is the **CLOSEST** to the **MILKY WAY** galaxy.

Can you count how many zeroes are in 1,000,000,000 (one billion)?

**Can you use your finger to trace the butterfly shape of the Bug Nebula?**

**FAR, FAR AWAY**

# NEBULA

Stars are born, or form, and last for billions of years. When they lose energy, they die.

When some kinds of stars die, they explode. All the leftover stardust is called a nebula.

New stars are born inside a nebula, too. Gases and dust pull together and form young stars.

The **HELIX NEBULA** looks like an eye.

This is how an ARTIST imagined light and other space objects being pulled toward a BLACK HOLE.

**FAR, FAR AWAY**

# BLACK HOLES

At the center of the Milky Way galaxy there is a black hole.

Black holes are invisible—they cannot be seen. A black hole is an area of space with gravity so strong that anything too close to it cannot escape.

Not even light can escape from black holes. That is why we cannot see them.

There is a **BLACK HOLE** in the **MIDDLE OF MOST GALAXIES.**

Which of these things is invisible: your bed, the air you breathe, or your family's car?

# CHAPTER FIVE

Dust storm

Lightning

Shelter

Solar collectors

Someday astronauts may explore Mars.

# EXPLORING SPACE

107

**EXPLORING SPACE**

# ROCKETS

Astronauts and equipment need to ride on a rocket to reach space. The rocket blasts up into the air. That is called a launch.

The rocket has to reach a speed of more than seven miles a second to escape gravity.

Some rockets put satellites into orbit around Earth. Satellites can help make maps, connect cell phones, and send television signals.

**WEATHER SATELLITES** help us know if we should dress for rain, snow, or sunshine.

**EXPLORING SPACE**

# INTERNATIONAL SPACE STATION

The International Space Station (ISS) orbits Earth. It was built for astronauts to work and live for a few weeks or months.

Astronauts sometimes leave the ISS to work outside the station. They take a walk in space. There is no air in space, and it is very cold. So an astronaut wears a protective space suit.

The **ISS** is about the size of a **FOOTBALL FIELD.**

**Do you think it would be fun to wear a space suit and walk in space?**

Some of the LARGEST TELESCOPES on Earth are on TOP OF MOUNTAINS, where the air is CLEARER.

**EXPLORING SPACE**

# TELESCOPES

A telescope helps people see things that are too far away in space to see with only their eyes. When you look through a telescope, things seem closer and bigger.

Astronomers use huge, powerful telescopes to study space. You can use a much smaller telescope at home.

**Have you ever looked through binoculars or a telescope to see faraway things better?**

Hubble Space Telescope

A school bus–size telescope called the Hubble Space Telescope orbits Earth. The Hubble telescope has taken more than a million pictures of planets, stars, and galaxies since 1990. It took these space photos.

Red supergiant star

Cat's Eye Nebula

## EXPLORING SPACE

Flying above the atmosphere, the **HUBBLE** has an even **BETTER VIEW** of space than the telescopes on top of **MOUNTAINS**.

Mystic Mountain
Carina Nebula

In 2018, a new telescope will take the place of Hubble. It is called the James Webb Space Telescope. It will be able to see farther and more clearly than Hubble can.

Astronomers have discovered thousands of **PLANETS ORBITING STARS** beyond our solar system.

Some planets in other solar systems have **TWO SUNS.**

Imaginary planet

**EXPLORING SPACE**

# GOLDILOCKS ZONE

Scientists wonder whether there is any other planet that has life on it.

They are looking for other planets like Earth that are in a "Goldilocks zone." That means the planet is just the right distance from its star so that it is neither too hot nor too cold. It is in the right place to have life.

There are probably many planets in Goldilocks zones outside our solar system.

**NASA found a PLANET FAR, FAR AWAY that is in a Goldilocks zone.**

**Do you know the story of "Goldilocks and the Three Bears"?** (Goldilocks liked things that were "just right.")

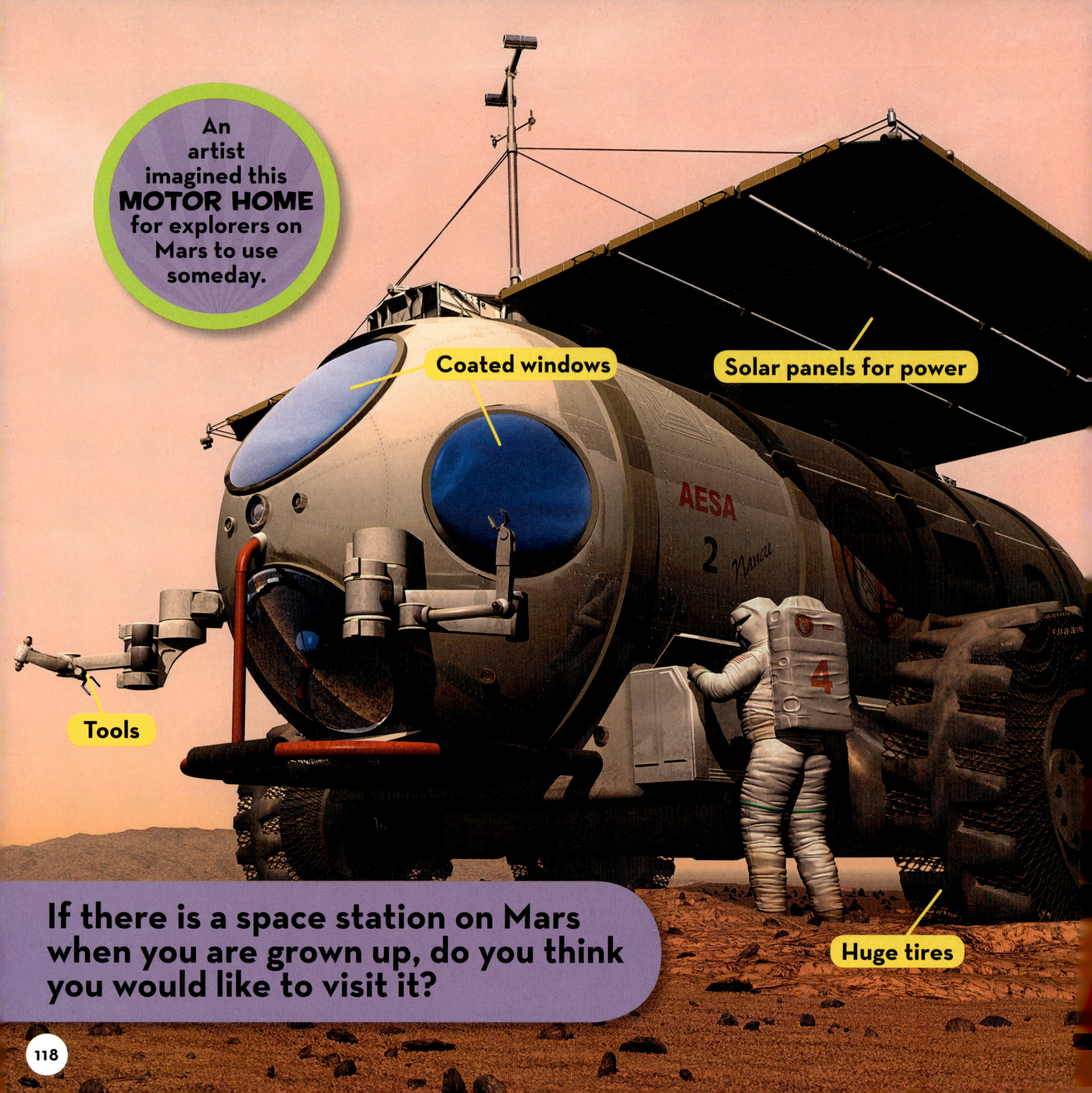

**EXPLORING SPACE**

# LIVING ON MARS?

Scientists think that someday people will visit Mars. But that won't happen for a very long time.

This is a **VIRGIN GALACTIC** spacecraft on a test flight over **CALIFORNIA**.

Before that, people like you may be able to travel into space in a spacecraft that looks like an airplane!

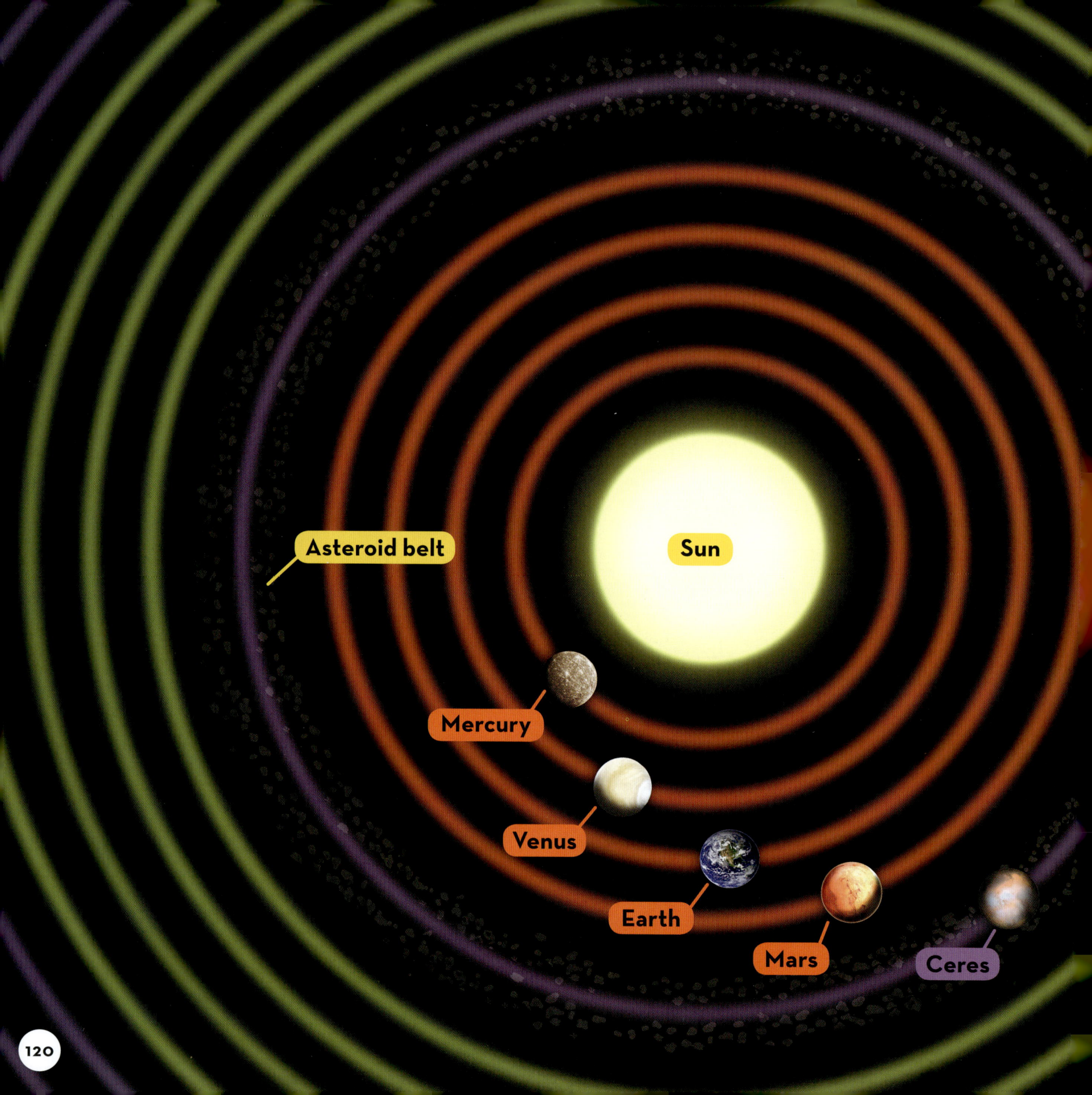

# SOLAR SYSTEM MAP

**U**se this diagram to see the order of the planets and dwarf planets in orbit around the sun. The planet sizes are not to scale.

### ROCKY PLANETS
Mercury

Venus

Earth

Mars

### GAS GIANTS
Jupiter

Saturn

Uranus

Neptune

### DWARF PLANETS
Ceres

Pluto

Haumea

Makemake

Eris

121

## PARENT TIPS

**Extend your child's experience** beyond the pages of this book. A visit to a planetarium is one great way to continue satisfying your child's curiosity about space. Here are some other activities you can do with *National Geographic Little Kids First Big Book of Space*.

### SUNRISE, SUNSET (TRACKING)

The sun is a star. Reinforce the concepts of sunrise and sunset by watching the movement of the sun across the sky on a bright, sunny day. Watch sunrise with your child, pointing out that you are looking toward the east. Go outside with your child mid-morning, at noon, and mid-afternoon. In the evening, watch the sunset. Each time, point out the change in the sun's position, and talk about how the sun sets in the west and rises in the east.

### DAY AND NIGHT (EXPERIMENTING)

Earth spins like a top. In a dimmed room, have your child hold a flashlight, pretending to be the sun. Draw a dot or tape a piece of paper on one spot on a ball or globe to represent the spot where you live. Then show your child how Earth spins on its axis, resulting in day (when the dot faces the sun) and night (when the dot has spun away from the sun). Then trade places, letting your child be Earth as you shine the "sun" on the ball.

### PHASES OF THE MOON (NATURE JOURNAL)

To experience the phases of the moon, your child will practice patience! Find out when the next crescent moon will occur in your area. Point out the banana-shaped moon and help your child draw the shape on a calendar. Every few nights, have your child notice the shape of the moon as it "grows" and "shrinks," marking the new shape on the calendar each time. The complete list of eight moon phases (four are described in the book on pages 26–27) is as follows: new moon, waxing crescent, first quarter, waxing gibbous, full moon, waning gibbous, last quarter, waning crescent. When the moon is full, have a full moon celebration by making moon pies or another round treat!

### THE MOON CLOSE-UP (USING BINOCULARS)

If you have a telescope, help your child use it to look at the moon. If not, you can use binoculars. Your child's viewing experience will be best if you can brace the binoculars, preferably with a tripod. Ask your child to describe the appearance of the moon and compare it to what is visible with the naked eye.

## SHOOTING STARS
### (OBSERVATION)
During August and December, the Perseid and Geminid meteor showers provide the best chance of seeing shooting stars. If you and your little one are game for this nighttime adventure, watch the news or check Internet astronomy sites to determine the best time to watch for the peak of a meteor shower. Lie down on a big blanket outside and enjoy the show!

## PLAY "CONCENTRATION"
### (MEMORY)
There are eight major planets and five dwarf planets. Make a deck of planet cards with your child. Use large index cards so there is room to draw on them. Help your child make two cards for each of the planets. On one side of each card, have her draw the planet. Use this book to reinforce unique things about each planet that she can add to each drawing. Help her write all their names: Mercury, Venus, Earth, Mars, Jupiter, Saturn, Uranus, Neptune, Ceres, Pluto, Haumea, Eris, and Makemake. Then play the card game "Concentration."

## DOT TO DOT
### (COUNTING)
Constellations are imaginary dot-to-dot pictures in the sky. Make a page of numbered dots and have your child practice connecting the numbers in order.

## STAR LIGHT
### (POETRY)
Teach your child this popular poem:

*Star light, star bright,
First star I see tonight,
I wish I may, I wish I might,
Have the wish I wish tonight.*

Encourage him to make a wish. Use the opportunity to have a conversation about wishes. Talk about the difference between "just for fun" wishes ("I wish I could fly!") and realistic ones ("I wish I could go to the playground!").

## STORY TIME
### (STORYTELLING)
The planet Earth is in a Goldilocks zone. Read the story "Goldilocks and the Three Bears" out loud. Then suggest that your child write a "book" about visiting a newly discovered planet in a Goldilocks zone. Have her dictate the story as you write and illustrate the book by drawing pictures on each page. Have her draw a cover and write a title for her book.

# GLOSSARY

**ASTERISM**
a group of stars that is smaller than a constellation

**ASTEROID**
a small, rocky space object

**ASTEROID BELT**
the area between Mars and Jupiter where most asteroids are found in orbit around the sun

**ASTRONAUT**
a person who travels into space

**ASTRONOMER**
a person who studies space

**ATMOSPHERE**
air surrounding a planet

**CALLISTO**
(kah-LIS-toe) one of the four largest moons orbiting Jupiter

**COMET**
a space object with a large orbit around the sun, made up of icy gases, rock, and dust

**CONSTELLATION**
one of 88 groupings of stars that make an imaginary picture

**DEIMOS**
(DIE-mas) one of two moons orbiting Mars

**DWARF PLANET**
a kind of small planet, including Ceres, Pluto, Haumea, Makemake, and Eris

**EUROPA**
(yoo-RO-pah) one of the four largest moons orbiting Jupiter

**FLYBY**
the flight of a spacecraft that passes by a planet, moon, or other space object

**GALAXY**
a very large group of stars, gas, and dust held together by gravity

**GANYMEDE**
(GAN-uh-meed) one of the four largest moons orbiting Jupiter

**GRAVITY**
the strong, invisible force that, for example, keeps things from floating off Earth into the sky

**GREAT DARK SPOT**
a huge storm on Neptune detected by Voyager 2 in 1989, which was no longer evident in Hubble photographs taken in 1994

**GREAT RED SPOT**
a huge storm on Jupiter

**IO**
(EYE-oh) one of the four largest moons orbiting Jupiter

**KUIPER BELT**
an area of space beyond Neptune

**LANDER**
a spacecraft that lands on the surface of a planet, moon, or other space object

**LAVA**
rock that comes from a volcano

**METEOR**
chunk of space rock that burns as it travels through Earth's atmosphere; sometimes called a shooting star

**METEORITE**
chunk of space rock (meteor) that reaches Earth's surface

**MOON**
a natural object that orbits a planet

**MOON PHASES**
the eight changing, sunlit views of the moon as it orbits Earth: new, waxing crescent, first quarter, waxing gibbous, full, waning gibbous, last quarter, waning crescent

**NASA**
National Aeronautics and Space Administration, the space program for the United States

**NEBULA**
cloud of stardust from exploded stars

**NEREID**
(NEER-ee-id) third largest moon orbiting Neptune

**ORBIT**
the path through space around a planet or star

**ORBITER**
a spacecraft that stays in orbit around a planet, moon, or other object in space without landing

**PHOBOS**
(FO-bis) one of two moons orbiting Mars

**PLANET**
a large, round object that orbits a star

**PROTEUS**
(PRO-tee-us) second largest moon orbiting Neptune

**PROXIMA-CENTAURI**
(PROK-suh-ma sen-TOR-eye) the second closest star to Earth

**ROCKET**
a powerful spacecraft that lifts astronauts and satellites and other equipment into space

**SATELLITE**
a spacecraft that orbits a planet and is filled with equipment to do jobs such as tracking weather and making maps

**SHOOTING STAR**
a nickname for a meteor as it burns in Earth's atmosphere

**SOLAR FLARE**
a sudden explosion in the sun's atmosphere

**SOLAR SYSTEM**
a star and the objects that orbit it

**STAR**
a bright, shining ball of gases such as Earth's sun, usually seen in the night sky

**SUN**
the star that is the center of Earth's solar system

**SUNGRAZER**
a comet that crashes into the sun

**SUNRISE**
the time when the sun appears in the sky in the morning

**SUNSET**
the time when the sun disappears from sight in the sky in the evening

**TELESCOPE**
a piece of equipment, usually shaped like a tube, that makes faraway things look closer

**TRITON**
(TRI-ton) largest moon orbiting Neptune

**UNIVERSE**
everything in space

# CREDITS

All artwork by David Aguilar unless otherwise noted below.

1, kentoh/Shutterstock; 7, NASA; 14, Zhabska Tetyana/Shutterstock; 15, ESA/NASA/SOHO; 16, Sergej Khakimullin/Shutterstock; 17 (left), djgis/Shutterstock; 17 (right), Dan Briški/Shutterstock; 18, David Aguilar; 19, John Wheeler/Alamy; 20 (top), Felix Mizioznikov/Shutterstock; 20 (bottom), Ocean/Corbis; 21 (left), Vasiliy Koval/Shutterstock; 21 (right), Toncsi/Shutterstock; 22, ZouZou/Shutterstock; 23, Frans Lanting/National Geographic Stock; 25 (left), Dennis Hallinan/Alamy; 26 (left), Yarygin/Shutterstock; 26 (right), Bruce Heinemann/Getty Images; 27 (left), Thom Gourley/age fotostock/Getty Images; 27 (right), Radius Images/Getty Images; 28 (left), NASA; 29, NASA; 31, Detlev van Ravenswaay/Photo Researchers, Inc.; 37 (left), Stocktrek Images/Getty Images; 38, NASA; 39, NASA; 41 (left), Photo Researchers/Getty Images; 42, NASA; 43, NASA/JPL; 45 (left), NASA/JPL; 46 (top left), NASA/JPL-Caltech/University of Arizona; 46 (bottom left), NASA/JPL-Caltech/University of Arizona; 46 (right), Stocktrek Images/Getty Images; 47, Stocktrek Images/Getty Images; 48 (top), NASA/JPL; 48 (bottom), NASA/JPL/Cornell; 49, NASA/JPL/Caltech; 52, NASA; 53 (top left), NASA; 53 (top right), NASA; 53 (bottom), NASA; 54, NASA/JPL; 55, NASA/JPL; 57 (left), Ludek Pesek/National Geographic Stock; 58, Steve A. Munsinger/Photo Researchers, Inc.; 60, NASA/JPL; 61 (left), Atlas Photo Bank/Photo Researchers, Inc.; 61 (right), NASA/ESA; 63 (bottom left), NASA; 63 (bottom right), NASA/JPL; 64, Stocktrek Images/Getty Images; 65 (left), Stocktrek Images/Getty Images; 65 (right), NASA; 69, NASA; 73, NASA/Johns Hopkins Applied Physics Laboratory; 74, NASA/JPL-Caltech; 80, Mark Garlick/Photo Researchers, Inc.; 81, NASA/Johns Hopkins University Applied Physics Laboratory/Southwest Research Institute; 86, ESA/AFP/Getty Images; 87, Erik Viktor/AFP/Getty Images; 90, NASA/JPL-Caltech/STScI/Institut d'Astrophysique; 91, NASA/JPL-Caltech; 92, NASA/ESA; 94, BestPhotoByMonikaGniot/Shutterstock; 95, Julian Baum/Photo Researchers, Inc.; 96, Amana Images Inc./Alamy; 97, Science Source/Photo Researchers/Getty Images; 98, NASA/ESA/STScI; 98 (right), StockCube/Shutterstock; 99 (left), NASA/ESA/STScI/AURA; 99 (right), NASA/ESA/STScI; 100, Babak Tafreshi/Photo Researchers, Inc.; 101, NG Maps/National Geographic Stock; 102, NASA; 103, NASA/ESA/Hubble SM4 ERO Team; 108, NASA/Darrell L. McCall; 108 (inset), NASA/JPL-Caltech; 109, Andrea Danti/Shutterstock; 110, NASA; 111, NASA/National Geographic Stock; 112, David Robertson/Alamy; 113, Steve Cole/iStockphoto; 114 (top), NASA/STScI; 114 (bottom left), NASA/AURA/STScI; 114 (bottom right), NASA/ESA/HEIC/STScI/AURA; 115, NASA/ESA/STScI; 118, Stocktrek Images/Getty Images; 119, David Paul Morris/Bloomberg/Getty Images

# INDEX

**Boldface** indicates illustrations.

## A
Andromeda (galaxy) 101
Asterisms 97, 124
Asteroid belt **8**, 73, **120-121**, 124
Asteroids **70-71**, **72**, 73, 75, **76**, 124
Astronauts
    definition 124
    on International Space Station 110, **110**, 111
    on Mars **106-107**, 118
    on moon 28, 29, **29**
    rockets 109
Atlas V (rocket) 108, **108**
Atmosphere 29, 124

## B
Big Dipper (asterism) 96, **96**, **97**
Black holes **104**, 105
Bug Nebula **102**

## C
Callisto (Jupiter's moon) 53, **53**, 124
Cassini (spacecraft) **60**, 60-61
Cat's Eye Nebula **114**
Ceres (dwarf planet) **8**, **76**, 77, 81, **120-121**
Charon (Pluto's moon) **78**, 80, **80**
Comets **84-87**, 124
Constellations 96, **96**, 97, **97**, 123, 124
Cool stars **92**, 93, **93**
Craters 39, **39**
Curiosity (rover) 49, **49**, 108, **108**
Cygnus (ellation) **96**

## D
Dactyl (Ida's moon) 75
Dawn (spaceship) **74**, 75, 77, 81
Daytime **16**, 16-17, **17**, 20, **20**, 122
Deimos (Mars's moon) **44**, 46, **46**, 124
Dione (Saturn's moon) **58**
Dwarf planets **76-83**, 123, 124

## E
Earth (planet) **18-23**
    distance to sun 13
    in galaxy 101, **101**
    gravity 22
    life 23, **23**
    meteors and meteorites 30, 31, **31**
    oceans **18**
    orbit 14, **14**, 19, **120-121**
    size **15**, 18
    in solar system **8**, **14**, **34**
    spinning 19, 20, 43, 62
    tilt 20, 21
Elliptical galaxies 99, **99**
Eris (dwarf planet) **9**, 83, **83**, **120-121**
Eros (asteroid) **73**
Europa (Jupiter's moon) 52, **52**, 53, 124
Exploring space **106-119**

## F
Flyby 60, 124

## G
Galaxies **98-101**, 124
Galileo (spaceship) 54, **54**
Ganymede (Jupiter's moon) 53, **53**, 124
Gas giants 35
Goldilocks zone 116, **116**, 117, 123
Gravity 22, 124
Great Dark Spot, Neptune **66**, 67, 124
Great Red Spot, Jupiter 50, **50**, 51, 124

## H
Haumea (dwarf planet) **9**, **82**, 83, **120-121**
Helix Nebula 103, **103**
Hi'iaka (Haumea's moon) **82**, 83
Hot stars **92**, 93, **93**
Hubble Space Telescope 114, **114**, 115
Huygens (lander) 61, **61**

## I
Iapetus (Saturn's moon) **58**
Ida (asteroid) 75
International Space Station (ISS) **110**, 111, **111**
Io (Jupiter's moon) 53, **53**, 124
Iron 45, **45**
Irregular galaxies 99, **99**

## J
Jaguars 23, **23**
James Webb Space Telescope 115
Juno (spacecraft) 55, **55**
Jupiter (planet) **50-55**
    atmosphere 50
    facts 51
    Great Red Spot 50, **50**, 51, 124
    moons **52**, 52-53, **53**, 124
    orbit 51, **120-121**
    in solar system **8**, **34**
    spaceships to **54**, 54-55, 55

## K
Kuiper belt
    comets **84**, 86
    definition 124
    dwarf planets 79, 83
    in solar system **9**

## L
Landers (spacecraft) 61, **61**, 124
Lunar roving vehicle 29, **29**

## M
Maat Mons, Venus 43, **43**
Magellan (spacecraft) **42**, 42-43
Makemake (dwarf planet) **9**, 83, **83**, **120-121**
Mars (planet) **44-49**
    exploration **106-107**
    facts 45
    iron 45, **45**
    living on 118, **118**, 119
    moons **44**, 46, **46**
    orbit **120-121**
    rovers 48, **48**, 49, **49**
    in solar system **8**, **34**
    volcanoes 44
Mercury (planet) **36-39**
    facts 37
    orbit 37, **120-121**
    in solar system **8**, **34**
    spaceships to 38, **38**, 39
MESSENGER (spaceship) 38, **38**, 39
Meteors and meteorites **30**, 31, **31**, 123, **124**
Milky Way (galaxy) 100, **100**, 101, **101**, 105

# INDEX

Miranda (Uranus's moon) **64,** 65, **65**
Moon **18, 24-29,** 30
    comparisons **37, 41**
    definition 124
    facts 25
    lander 28, **28**
    lunar roving vehicle 29, **29**
    orbit 24, 25
    parent tips 122-123
    phases **26,** 26-27, **27,** 122, 124
    rising **10-11**
    shape 26-27
    surface **47**
Mystic Mountain Carina Nebula **115**

## N
Namaka (Haumea's moon) **82,** 83
National Aeronautics and Space Administration (NASA) 38, 124
Nebulae **90,** 103
    Bug Nebula **102**
    Cat's Eye Nebula **114**
    definition 124
    Helix Nebula 103, **103**
    Mystic Mountain Carina Nebula **115**
Neptune (planet) **66-69**
    facts 67
    Great Dark Spot **66,** 67, 124
    moons 68, **68,** 69
    orbit **120-121**
    in solar system 9, **34**
    spacecraft to 69, **69**
    weather 67
Nereid (Neptune's moon) 69, 124
New Horizons (spaceship) 81, **81**
Nighttime 17, **17,** 20, **20,** 122

## O
Opportunity (rover) 49
Orbiters (spacecraft) 60, 124
Orbits 14, 124

## P
Phobos (Mars's moon) **44,** 46, **46,** 124
Planets **32-69**
    definition 124
    Goldilocks zone 116, **116,** 117
    parent tips 123
Pluto (dwarf planet) **78-81**
    as dwarf planet 79
    facts 79
    moons 78, 80, **80**
    orbit 78, **120-121**
    in solar system 9
    spaceships to 81, **81**
    spinning 79
Proteus (Neptune's moon) 69, 124
Proxima-Centauri (star) 95, **95,** 124

## R
Red supergiant star **114**
Rhea (Saturn's moon) **58**
Rockets 108, **108,** 109, 124
Rocky planets 35
Rosetta (spacecraft) **86, 87**

## S
Satellites 109, **109,** 124
Saturn (planet) **56-61, 63**
    facts 57
    moons 58, **58,** 59, **59,** 61, **61**
    orbit **120-121**
    rings 56, 57, **57**
    in solar system 9, **34**
    spacecraft to **60,** 60-61, **61**
Shooting stars 30, **30,** 123, 124
Sojourner (rover) 48, **48**
Solar collectors **106**
Solar flare **12,** 125
Solar system **8-9,** 9, 13, 125
Space suits 29, **29, 110, 110,** 111
Spiral galaxies 98, **98,** 99, 101, 101
Spirit (rover) **48,** 49
Stars **88-89, 92-97**
    constellations 96, **96,** 97, **97,** 123, 124
    definition 125
    parent tip 123
    Proxima-Centauri 95, **95,** 124
    red supergiant **114**
    temperatures **92,** 93, 93
Summer 21, **21**
Sun **12-17**
    cautions about 17
    definition 125
    distance from Earth 13
    setting **10-11**
    size 15, **15**
    solar flare **12,** 125
    in solar system **8-9,** 9, **34**
    sunlight **16,** 16-17, **17,** 94, **94**
Sungrazers (comets) 85, 125
Sunrise 16, **16,** 122, 125
Sunset 17, **17,** 122, 125

## T
Telescopes **112-115,** 125
Tethys (Saturn's moon) **58**
Titan (Saturn's moon) **58,** 59, **59,** 61, **61**

Triton (Neptune's moon) 68, **68,** 125

## U
Universe **90,** 90-91, **91,** 125
Uranus (planet) **62-65**
    facts 63
    moons **64,** 65, **65**
    orbit 62, **120-121**
    in solar system 9, **34**
    spacecraft to 65, 69, **69**
    spinning 62
Ursa Major (constellation) **96**

## V
Venus (planet) **40-43**
    facts 41
    in night sky 41, **41**
    orbit **120-121**
    in solar system **8, 34**
    spaceships to 42, **42**
    spinning 42, 43
    volcano 43, **43**
Vesta (asteroid) **74,** 75
Virgin Galactic (spacecraft) 119, **119**
Volcanoes
    Io 53
    lava 124
    Mars 44
    Triton 68, **68**
Venus 43, **43**
Voyager 2 (spacecraft) 65, 69, **69**

## W
Weather satellites 109, **109**
Winter 21, 21

# FOR TYLER AND ALEXA, IN MEMORY OF THEIR LOVING GRANDMOTHER, NANCY JO, WHO WAS A BRIGHT, SHINING STAR IN THE LIVES OF ALL WHO KNEW HER. — CDH

Published by Collins
An imprint of HarperCollins Publishers
1 Robroyston Gate,
Glasgow
G33 1JN
www.harpercollins.co.uk

HarperCollins Publishers
Macken House
39/40 Mayor Street Upper
Dublin 1
D01 C9W8
Ireland

© 2012 National Geographic Partners LLC. All rights reserved.
NATIONAL GEOGRAPHIC KIDS and Yellow Border Design are trademarks of National Geographic Society, used under license.

First published 2012
This edition 2026

ISBN 9780008825300

10 9 8 7 6 5 4 3 2 1

All rights reserved. No part of this publication may be reproduced, stored in a retrieval system, or transmitted, in any form or by any means, electronic, mechanical, photocopying, recording or otherwise without the prior permission in writing of the publisher and copyright owners.

Without limiting the exclusive rights of any author, contributor or the publisher of this publication, any unauthorised use of this publication to train generative artificial intelligence (AI) technologies is expressly prohibited. HarperCollins also exercise their rights under Article 4(3) of the Digital Single Market Directive 2019/790 and expressly reserve this publication from the text and data mining exception.

The contents of this publication are believed correct at the time of printing. Nevertheless the publisher can accept no responsibility for errors or omissions, changes in the detail given or for any expense or loss thereby caused.

HarperCollins does not warrant that any website mentioned in this title will be provided uninterrupted, that any website will be error free, that defects will be corrected, or that the website or the server that makes it available are free of viruses or bugs. For full terms and conditions please refer to the site terms provided on the website.

A catalogue record for this book is available from the British Library

Printed in India

If you would like to comment on any aspect of this book, please contact us at the above address or online.
natgeokidsbooks.co.uk
collins.reference@harpercollins.co.uk

**Acknowledgments**
A special thanks to James L. Green, Ph.D., and Steven H. Williams, Ph.D., of the National Aeronautics and Space Administration's Planetary Science Division in Washington, D.C. Their time and expertise were invaluable in the preparation of this book.

**Prepared by the Book Division**
Hector Sierra,
*Senior Vice President and General Manager*

Nancy Laties Feresten,
*Senior Vice President, Editor in Chief, Children's Books*

Jonathan Halling,
*Design Director, Books and Children's Publishing*

Jay Sumner,
*Director of Photography, Children's Publishing*

Jennifer Emmett,
*Editorial Director, Children's Books*

Eva Absher-Schantz,
*Managing Art Director, Children's Publishing*

Carl Mehler,
*Director of Maps*

R. Gary Colbert,
*Production Director*

Jennifer A. Thornton,
*Director of Managing Editorial*

**Staff for This Book**
Robin Terry, *Project Manager*
Catherine D. Hughes, *Project Editor*
David M. Seager, *Art Director*
Ruthie Thompson, *Production Designer*
Lori Epstein, *Senior Illustrations Editor*
Annette Kiesow, *Illustrations Editor*
Sharon Thompson, *Researcher*
Kate Olesin, *Assistant Editor*
Kathryn Robbins, *Design Production Assistant*
Hillary Moloney, *Illustrations Assistant*
Grace Hill, *Associate Managing Editor*
Joan Gossett, *Production Editor*
Lewis R. Bassford, *Production Manager*
Susan Borke, *Legal and Business Affairs*

**Manufacturing and Quality Management**
Phillip L. Schlosser, *Senior Vice President*
Chris Brown, *Vice President, NG Book Manufacturing*
George Bounelis, *Vice President, Production Services*
Nicole Elliott, *Manager*
Rachel Faulise, *Manager*
Robert L. Barr, *Manager*